THE NEXTGEN TRUSTED ADVISOR

How to create value through trust based relationships

Nadeem Ladha

Pitch It Advisory

CONTENTS

Title Page
Chapter 1: Purpose of this book — 1
Chapter 2: Trust in the modern world is a differentiator — 5
Chapter 3: What is a trusted advisor and why would you want to become one? — 9
Chapter 4: Know yourself first! — 16
Chapter 5: What type of relationship are you creating? — 20
Chapter 6: Getting to know your client — 23
Chapter 7: The relationship contract — 28
Chapter 8: Sell the relationship, not the product — 35
Chapter 9: Understand your client's agenda — 40
Chapter 10: It's about give and take — 45
Chapter 11: Your client's personality does matter — 55
Chapter 12: Be present, be relevant — 62
Chapter 13: Create, grow and share your network — 68
Chapter 14: Be open, be personal, be a friend — 75
Chapter 15: Credibility — 82
Chapter 16: Creative meetings — 86
Chapter 17: Go out and build trusted relationships — 93

CHAPTER 1: PURPOSE OF THIS BOOK

Advisors benefit greatly from the ability to connect with other people. In order to be a trusted advisor, you must be able to understand and empathise with the people you are trying to help. Only then can you hope to offer them the best possible advice.

This book is designed to help you become a trusted advisor. In it, you'll learn how to connect with others, how to understand their needs, and how to give them the best possible advice. You'll also learn how to build trust and credibility with your clients.

A trusted advisor aims to empathise, to understand, to coach, to interpret and then to solve an issue that their client has. If you're ready to become a trusted advisor, then this book is for you.

Let's reflect a little on the how patterns have changed over time in advisors' behaviours, and the business models in which they have operated over the past few decades. This will explain why the trusted advisor breed has died out in favour of short term focused salesman.

As businesses grew and became multi-national and then global, consulting evolved into a very profitable industry. Those who knew how to successfully apply their technical knowhow to business problems were in high demand and could command sizeable fees for their services. These advisory firms started off small, and so every consultant needed to earn their clients' trust to be successful.

As advisory businesses became more common, the larger advisory firms could rely on their brands and a handful of "salesmen" to get more revenue rather than ensuring that all of their people were building their own strong relationships. Senior and well paid advisors became mostly market facing and junior workers were left to do the grunt work. Those businesses valued winning work the most and quickly promoted the advisors that won work consistently. The long term nature of relationships wasn't tested in this new environment, but of course as more senior advisors were put into client facing roles, they had all the opportunities to succeed whilst everyone else had few. It became a self fulfilling prophecy that this approach created a business model that focused on short term relationships, sidelined junior team members and rewarded salesman disproportionately to prevent them going elsewhere.

With more organisations competing and lowering their prices, many turned to a model that stressed the number of hours spent working at a desk. This meant that junior consultants' people skills were neglected in favour of speed and efficiency. This has rapidly intensified over the past decade, and as a result, the quality of advisor-client relationships has decreased.

The pressure on consultants to find and sell their next project has never been higher. In order to meet their targets, they have less time to truly get to know their clients and understand their needs. As a result, they often provide overpriced advice that is neither helpful nor trustworthy, and usually requires multiple iterations to get right as up front time with the client has been neglected.

This book is designed to help you break this cycle. In it, you'll learn how to focus on building long term relationships that create real value - financially and through personal satisfaction.

At a lot of firms, consulting is becoming more transactional in nature. The focus is on the bottom line - how much revenue can be generated - rather than on developing long-term relationships with clients.

When we look at training programmes at consulting firms in the early stages of employees' careers, there is a huge amount of "on the job" training and training on technical expertise. However, there is very limited training on consulting skills, apart from lip service in the form of the odd soft skills course.

The result is that many consultants do not know how to build trust, how to have in-depth, or strategic conversations or how to develop long-term relationships.

The message from most advisory firms to their employees is unfortunately very clear. Become a technical expert first and spend all of your time - indeed all of your unpaid overtime on billable work. Developing relationships is something that you will learn to do later if you're lucky.

This is the wrong approach. If you want to be a trusted advisor, your firm and all of its consultants should prioritise developing strong relationships with clients from the very beginning. The reality is that real consulting skills, real advisory ability is the foundation of delivering the best outcomes. It is also the key to sustaining long-term relationships with clients.

Let's think about this. If more time was spent on talking pre-engagement, understanding the real issues, not just the technical problem - outcomes would be better, solutions would be quicker, trust would be stronger as you'd always deliver and work with your clients as a team. Margins would actually be higher because the advisor understands the complexity of the client and their business and therefore understands the outcomes that need to be delivered.

The focus on the technical aspects of a project often means that the human element is neglected. In order to be a trusted advisor, you need to be able to understand and empathise with your client's situation.

The lack of human interaction through the advisory process when you begin a consulting career is staggeringly poor judgement by management who focus on utilisation to improve margin, rather than adding value to their clients. It results in a disengaged pool of resource, rather than engaged and happy people that understand that the value of their work comes from solving people's problems, not just finding a technically right answer.

This is why I have written this book. This book aims to tell consultants in the first few years of their career, how to focus on becoming trusted advisors, not just technically excellent cogs in a large consulting machine. This book also represents hope. Hope that these same consultants will become future leaders within our advisory firms, and that they will remember the importance of human relationships when they get there.

If you are a consultant, or thinking about becoming one, I hope this book will give you some useful insights into how to develop strong relationships with your clients and become a trusted advisor.

CHAPTER 2: TRUST IN THE MODERN WORLD IS A DIFFERENTIATOR

It is a fallacy of modern day thinking that capital is the primary enabler of activity, commerce and growth in the broader economy. The primary enabler, the one single factor that underpins the outcome regarding whether activities will happen or indeed whether money fundamentally has any value, is trust.

Organisations tend to assume that they can take trust for granted, as many activities are formalised legally in a way which penalises the breaking of a contract once it has been agreed. However, no legal documents, no penalties, indeed no informal agreements can ever be made without there first being a level of real trust between people, between organisations or even merely the trust that an outcome benefits both parties that agreed to participate in an activity.

There are still many cultures situations where family ties, networks, friendships and even good old-fashioned loyalties trump legal contracts. Within the last ten years, I have seen formal signs documents torn up with no legal recourse either because jurisdiction makes recourse difficult, or because people realise that sometimes the personal bond is greater and than ink on paper.

We still live in a world where trust dictates who gets selected to help with a problem, where the person who has delivered before gets to deliver again and again, and reputation and honesty and openness create the perfect relationship between buyer and seller or between decision maker and advisor. The difference is a buyer of goods is usually able to see and test the goods before payment and delivery. The only aspect that a decision maker has before choosing his advisor is the promise of a good outcome (ie the trust between them) and price. Given that advice is rarely a commodity, price can and regularly does fall out of the equation, and this leaves us with only trust.

People might argue that experience and reputation are also important in a decision-makers choice of their advisors. I'd absolutely agree, but all of these elements combined together are part of the trust equation. More specifically, it is easier to trust an advisor that is experienced, that has a good reputation and if his network backs them up.

In a world dominated scale enabled by speed and technology, we have created expectations of more sales for less work, and where value can be created through the commoditisation, often not just products, but services as well. Real trust is becoming an even rarer commodity and therefore extremely valuable for those advisors that understand that trust still underpins every relationship and every transaction. Even the use of the word "transaction" reinforces the image of exchanging money for something that is definable. In the advisory world, not falling into the trap of trying to breakdown everything into bullet points of deliverables, is the key to ensuring and that advice remains about the ideas, the people, the solutions and the outcomes. Fundamentally good outcomes which help people based on good ideas is the fuel that builds trust, and as we all see in the later chapters, trust is the key to being a successful advisor and not just a successful commodity salesman.

Whether you are looking for products or services, a bespoke solution tailored for a specific situation and a particular person is always worth more than an off-the-shelf product. It isn't just the additional amount of time that is needed to create a bespoke product that people value and therefore are willing to pay more for. Whether it is clothing, holidays or advice, people like been treated as individuals because that is the essence of being human. A bespoke service or product also gives the buyer a better outcome, a tailored outcome that fits much better. As such in order to trust bespoke advice, a buyer needs to trust the creator of that advice - i.e. the advisor.

And so, if we accept that it is becoming harder to stand out in a mass-market world, where even advice is commoditised and sold as a product, deep relationships and trust can be used as a differentiator. This makes a huge amount of sense. The buyer of advice, usually a senior decision maker is seeking advice because they haven't got the knowledge, expertise or time to solve the problem themselves. However, if the problem still needs solving, it must be materially important to them. One can conclude therefore that the problem is complex and is likely to have materially serious consequences if the right answer isn't found. If there is a serious issue in your house that you cannot DIY and fix yourself, it is unlikely that you will trust an off-the-shelf solution without a trusted advisor to reassure you or to help you navigate through the complex issue. The decision maker needs, or at least feels they need, reassurance from someone they trust and tailored advice from someone who can deliver. This is why when you find a builder, plumber, electrician, tailor or architect that has a trusted personal brand, they are in demand, they are rare, they are valuable and therefore they are paid the most - it is no different in the consulting industry.

Let's for a minute dig a little bit deeper into the psyche of the senior decision maker who has a problem, and why trust is so critical to them when considering who they should ask to help them out. Ultimately the first level of trust is the confidence that the advisor will be able to deliver. Ultimately, the CFO or CEO or MD needs to know that the problem will be solved with certainty and within the time parameters that they are operating under. Without this certainty, the problem will continue to be a distraction, and one which and they know and they themselves can not solve without relying heavily on somebody else. By asking an advisor to take on the problem, they are taking responsibility for the outcome and they will be held accountable by their board and by the shareholders if the problem isn't solved. Therefore the decision maker is trusting their chosen advisor with their own reputation and probably with some of their remuneration!

The next level of trust is much deeper and exists because, suddenly, the decision maker must accepts loss of control. Ultimately they still have full ownership of the consequences and they are probably used to performing at a very high-level. They are probably also very aware that by subcontracting the problem to an advisor, they will lose visibility for significant periods of time whilst the problem is being fixed. Although the adviser cannot hand back control, they can hand back visibility and they can also use the comfort that they will be giving the decision maker as a way to build even more trust within the relationship.

Finally, the client needs to trust that the advisor is equipped with experience, commerciality, a brilliant team, and a sense of commitment so that they can trust the guidance and the answers that are being proposed by the adviser without having to question the intricacies of the solution.

CHAPTER 3: WHAT IS A TRUSTED ADVISOR AND WHY WOULD YOU WANT TO BECOME ONE?

The Trusted Advisor is a term that was first coined by David Maister, Charles Green, and Robert M. Galford in their book of the same name. In it, they defined a trusted advisor as "someone who is looked to for advice and counsel because of his or her deep knowledge and experience, sound judgment, and ability to help clients make good decisions."

While the term "trusted advisor" is often used in business contexts, it can also be applied to our personal lives. We all have people whom we turn to for advice and guidance, whether it's a family member, friend, or mentor. These are the people we trust to give us honest feedback and help us make good decisions.

If you're looking to become a trusted advisor in your personal or professional life, there are certain qualities you need to possess. Let's take a look at some of the most important ones.

    1. Emotional intelligence: The ability to understand and control your emotions, as well as the ability to understand and navigate the emotions of others, is critical for becoming

a trusted advisor. This quality allows you to build trust and rapport with others, as well as navigate complex conversations.

2. Deep knowledge and experience: In order to offer sound advice, you need to have a deep understanding of the topic at hand. This comes from both formal education and real-world experience.

3. Good judgement: Trusted advisors are able to make sound judgement calls, based on their knowledge and experience. They know when to take risks and when to play it safe.

4. Ability to help clients make good decisions: A trusted advisor doesn't just offer advice, they also help their clients make good decisions. This involves actively listening to their clients, understanding their needs, and providing them with the information they need to make an informed decision.

5. Strong communication skills: Trusted advisors need to be able to communicate effectively, both in written and verbal form. They need to be able to clearly articulate their thoughts and ideas, in order to help their clients make the best possible decisions.

When I started my consulting career in 2002, I didn't understand the nuances of what it meant to be a trusted advisor. Over the past two decades, I have been both a technical advisor and a strategic advisor to many different clients across various industries and multiple geographies. I have also been a client buying advice from a whole range of advisors who help me look after billions of pounds of assets. I have seen and continue to see good advisors and bad advisors, but I can count on two hands those who I count as being my trusted advisors. Most of my budget is spent with these advisors and the firms they represent, because I know - I trust - that I'll get good outcomes. This is the most important thing to me.

About thirteen years into my advisory career, I reached a point when it became obvious to me that taking the next step meant more than being technical good, more than being commercial and more than being narrowly strategic with my clients.

To get to that next level, I needed to move past being an individual who is credible, reliable and innovative. I wasn't too sure how to achieve this because these were the very characteristics that had got me this far and had made me successful up to this point in my career.

What these talents enabled me to do, was to do a job like thousands of other people in my industry. I could do a great job for my clients, and look great to my business as someone that can deliver excellent advice. I was an expert, a specialist in my field and someone that could conjure up new ideas that solved some serious problems. But now I needed to be more.

I needed to do something that meant that clients valued me, not just for my technical expertise but for the value I brought to them as a person. I needed my personal brand to differentiate me from the noise of other experts like me so that I would stand out as being the obvious person that people in my network would call when they had a serious problem or knew someone that had a problem, or just wanted to float an idea past. How could I make them think of me?

I wish someone had told me how to be a successful and trusted advisor 20 years ago. I now know what I needed to do to get to the next level, and the level beyond that and then all the way to the top. Importantly, I now know how to do this and enjoy every minute of it, because in reality it's what I do best.

Yes, you need to be technically credible, you need to be reliable, but most of all you need to be trusted. To be trusted, you need to spend time and emotional energy building relationships. If someone had told me this 20 years ago and how to do it well, I would have had time to build 20 years of deep relationships with people that are now in very senior positions across a huge number of organisations - these relationships are the lifeblood of any successful consulting firm and of any successful consulting career.

This book represent the inflection point for me as a consultant. I have written it for those individuals that are like me in the middle of my advisory career, trying to take a successful career to the very top. It is also for those who are about to embark on their consulting careers or those that are in the first few years trying to understand how to make the most of their strengths in an industry where thousands of other talented people are trying to get to the top as well.

As such, I will start at the beginning and try to answer why so many consultants find themselves in the position that I found myself in.

A lot of business consulting careers start off technical in their nature. This is natural, because the one thing that all business consultancies need is technically gifted individuals who can solve complex problems. These technical individuals as they progress through their careers are slowly given non-technical responsibilities - people responsibilities, strategic responsibilities and the responsibility to win work. These opportunities tend to be scarce early on in a career as the need of the business at entry level is mostly a technical one. Technical excellence and time is what the business needs and demands and this is what is focussed on in training, in progress reviews and in reward discussions. Technical excellence is what gets you on to the exciting projects with major clients.

As their career develops these individuals become experts in their areas, specialists who are able to solve the most complex of problems. They may not be the best at communicating the solutions, and typically they are even less good at trying to understand a client's issues outside of their specialist areas.

However technically talented an individual might be, unless they are able to find a need for their own expertise and other expertise within their wider business, they will struggle to become the driving force of their business and the future leaders of their business.

What really drives the success of any consulting business are those individuals that are able to understand and leverage everyone else's expertise and find the need for this expertise in the market by understanding their clients' problems at the broadest level. Those individuals will bring together the knowledge, the people and the technology to solve these wide ranging problems.

Note that in the title of this book, I have used the word advisor and not salesman. It's worth spending a few moments distinguishing between the two because this is central to the philosophy of this book.

A salesman takes a product or solution out into the market and tries to find companies or people that need that product or solution. Most of the time the salesman has to convince the clients that they have a problem to start with all that the solution provides some of the kind of benefits whether that economic value, strategic value or time value. There is still value being created here, but it's not necessarily solving an urgent issue or addressing a top priority for the client.

The salesman only really cares about a specific set of problems and a specific set of products, solutions or competencies. Because a specific product or solution solves a specific problem, the relationship between the salesman and the client is unlikely to be very long or very deep. But the salesman cares about the sale and so this model suits them. Businesses that are narrow in their product offering need salesmen - double glazing, cars, real estate and furniture are good examples.

An advisor on the other hand finds people or companies and spends time understanding what their specific issues are, and then goes away to use the many tools at his or her disposal to help to solve their particular problems. A client will have a number of different issues over a long period of time and perhaps across a number of different companies over their career. Therefore the relationship between an advisor and the client is likely to be personal, long lasting and deep. The advisor cares about the client and will be the reason why a client becomes loyal to a certain consultancy or professional advisory firm. In reality, the client is loyal to the advisor. This loyalty is extremely valuable and that is why consulting firms will pay a lot to attract and retain consultants that demonstrate that they can leverage their relationships.

There is a lot of evidence to show that it is trusted relationships that generate maximum value for both the client and the advisor's firm. In particular large, complex, time-consuming and the most urgent issues are usually solved by people who have the strongest relationships. From a human nature perspective, this makes a lot of sense. If you have a really critical issue that you need to solve urgently and it must be done right, you will go to someone who you trust that can deliver the required outcome. You are less likely to spend the time comparing alternative solutions in the market or trying to negotiate a better price, because the problem needs to be solved quickly and it needs to be solved right. And the person that you trust the most is the person that you think can deliver for you and that has delivered for you in the past on many occasions.

Crucially, a salesman is selling a commodity, a product or a service that can be packaged up and sold multiple times. The less bespoke a service is, the cheaper it is.

An advisor provides themselves as the value proposition and may even give this value away for free recognising that his time and intellectual property will be paid for implementing the solution once the problem and the value of solving the problem has been articulated by the client. There's only one of them and so creating demand for a scarce resource, in this case a combination of trust, networks, experience, knowledge and time, does not lose its value as it cannot be easily copied and sold as long as the personal brand stands out sufficiently.

This book isn't about how to sell, there are tonnes of books that can help you to optimise your selling technique. This book is about developing your relationships so that you won't have to sell, so that your relationships are strong enough having been built-in on the foundation of trust that clients will reach out to you when *they* have a problem. At some point in the near future and probably a good number of times over a period of years they will have a problem that they need help solving. And when they have a problem that is high on the priority list they'll want someone that they can trust. The trust that you have built up has value, and they will pay for that value.

But, becoming a trusted advisor takes time. It can be easy to fool yourself and others about the strength of a relationship. Be honest with yourself and identify those relationships where the relationship can be stronger. What you need to ask yourself is: Would the client call me first if they had an issue?

CHAPTER 4: KNOW YOURSELF FIRST!

To be a successful trusted advisor, you need to be able to add value to those you are advising. It makes sense that you can add most value by doing the things you are best at and enjoy the most. In order to do this, it is critical that you know what you're best at and align your advisory career and your client conversations with these strengths.

So, in becoming a trusted advisor you need to get to know yourself first. You need to understand your own strengths, weaknesses, values and motivations. This self-awareness will be the foundation upon which you build trust with others. Once you know what makes you tick, you can start to share this information with others in a way that will help them understand you better.

Being open and honest about who you are and what you stand for is an important part of gaining trust. People need to know that they can rely on you to be consistent in your words and actions. If you say one thing but do another, or if your behavior changes depending on who you're around, people will quickly lose faith in you.

Let's look at an example. You may be an strong innovator; somebody who loves creating ideas that your business colleagues or other advisors may not have thought of. But if you're not good at communicating these ideas or don't follow through on them, people will quickly lose faith in your ability to deliver. On the other hand, if you are able to share your ideas in a way that others can understand and see that you are committed to making them a reality, people will be more likely to trust you.

You might be a strategist or a futurist that can help people to think beyond the immediate issues. You may have an innate ability to help your clients that do not have this strength to help guide their business into the future. If you can share your ideas and help them to see the potential in these new markets, then you will build trust.

You may be an enabler who can join the dots and connect your client to the right person in your network. You may have a knack for asking the right questions that help your clients find their own solutions. You might be a sounding board for new ideas or for difficult conversations. These are all valuable strengths that can help you build trust with others. What is important here is not assuming that these discussions will immediately lead to a specific piece of work or opportunity. These discussions do more than that, they create emotional value, they create a bond and they create trust and they will mean that you get the call when something relevant does come up.

All of these strengths are valuable to different people and in different situations. Playing to your own strengths, once you know them yourself, will provide you with opportunities to shine. Trying to be good at something that you're average at, will lead to average outcomes and therefore average value generation.

The key is to be aware of your own strengths and weaknesses and to use this knowledge to build trust with others. When you are clear about what you bring to the table, you can be more confident in your interactions and conversations. This confidence will be evident to others and will help to build trust.

Your strengths become part of your personal brand. In your network you may be know as the person that comes up with radical ideas, or the individual that just gets things done. We will discuss your personal brand and the importance of this later on.

It is therefore important that your perceived strengths are truly your strengths, not ones that you think your preferred audience would want you to have. Your strengths might not necessarily be the strengths that are traditionally seen as the fun and exciting ones. You'll soon be found out, you'll be seen as average if you convince yourself that you are great at something that you are just OK at. More critically, you won't be able to tell the stories that will make that lasting impression. A lack of authenticity tends to lead to a lack of substance. And a lack of substance isn't memorable.

It's worth spending time making sure that you know your strengths. Once you are clear about these, focus on building your personal brand around them. This is what will make you memorable and therefore more likely to be trusted by others.

Once you think you know what your strengths are, test out your thinking with your friends, with your family and with your colleagues and see whether they agree. Be open minded. Sometimes our strengths are the ones that come most naturally to us and we dont even realise that they are strengths. We might be good at something but not see it as a strength because we don't realise that we are better than average. This is very common. It is easy to assume that things that you find easy are easy to everyone. It is also easy to assume that everyone enjoys the things that you enjoy. You will be surprised at how often others feel uncomfortable doing the things that you find easy.

Make sure your colleagues know your strengths too. When they are considering who to ask for help on a project or an opportunity, you want them to think of you. If they dont know what your strengths are, they won't be able to make that connection.

One final point on strengths. It is important not only to focus on your personal strengths but also the collective strengths of your team. When you are thinking about how to add value to your clients, it is important to think about not only what you can do but also what your team can do. This allows you to present a comprehensive solution rather than just a partial one. It also helps build trust because it shows that you are thinking about the client's needs and not just your own.

So, in order to become a trusted advisor, get to know yourself first. Understand your own strengths and weaknesses and use this knowledge to build trust with others. Be clear about what you bring to the table and be confident in your interactions and conversations. This will help you shine in your role as a trusted advisor.

CHAPTER 5: WHAT TYPE OF RELATIONSHIP ARE YOU CREATING?

In the previous chapter, we discussed the importance of knowing your own strengths. When trying to build strong relationships, you also need to spend some time figuring out what types of relationships you want to form. What role do you wish to play in those relationships? Some examples might include being a specialist, a connector, a sounding board, or a facilitator. There are many more, but understanding this enables you to understand the dynamic of your relationships - and of course your role in the relationship is dependent on your strengths.

A lot of strong relationships in the business place evolve over time. The specialist manager at a consultancy firm is likely to form a relationship with a mid-level client. Over time, the client will get promoted through the ranks and will start to make more important decisions, and as long as the relationship is strong, then the trust between the consultant and the client will grow over time. When the client is at the peak of their career, they will bring the consultant with them. This may seem like a long game, but it's really important that a number of your relationships are formed in this way.

Sometimes you may have a choice about the nature of your

relationship with a client as it may not be defined by the work that you are already doing. For example, an introductory conversation may have been setup by a colleague or friend. This is a great opportunity to curate your own relationship.

In this situation you need to look at the dynamics of the situation to understand what kind of relationship would be most valuable to both parties. What kind of decisions does this individual make within their business? Do they influence someone in C-Suite? Are they C-Suite? Do they care about strategy or do they care about process? Are they a detailed person or do they get excited by innovation? Speak to the person that made the introduction to get some of this information.

You then have to look at yourself and what you can offer. Does the relationship help you to test ideas that you could take to someone else in their business? Are they able to take your suggestions to their boss or their peers? Are you able to give them the innovation that they need, or some strategic direction. Maybe they need clarity over process on a major project that they have been asked to lead or deliver? Of course, it may well be that you can't fulfil their needs, but can use your network to solve their problems instead?

In essence you will need to decide how the relationship between you two will work. How do both of you get value from the relationship now and in the long term. It doesn't really matter what relationship you decide on. Indeed, it will most likely evolve in the future into something completely different. Different people that you meet will need to form a different type relationship with you depending on their own needs and their own personality.

You'll need to be agile as their needs change. Your own needs will change too depending on your own responsibilities or point in your career lifecycle. When you talk about personal agenda, understand their vision for the next few months, then next few years but also beyond. Keep asking about their career goals and how you can help. Don't assume their goals are static - they won't be. What does their legacy look like? How about their family ambitions or geographical ambitions?

It's really important to understand that it takes two to form a relationship. It is not a one-way street. But at the start of the relationship, you'll need to offer something of value, and you should do this without any entitlement or expectation until it has been earned. Of course, it's not always possible to find a way to help each other out. But even in these situations, it's important to remember that the relationship is still valuable. It's still an opportunity to learn and to understand a different perspective.

Eventually you will end up with a whole portfolio of close and diverse relationships across different organisations and with different types of people. The more trusted relationships you have, the more powerful your network will become and the more people will come and ask you to be their specialist, to be their generalist, to be an introducer or to be their strategist.

Suddenly you'll find yourself having very similar conversations with lots of different people, and you'll be able to use the new ideas and information from all of these conversations in more and more conversations. These conversations will become richer, you will be more credible, and your brand become an extremely powerful and valuable asset to you and your business.

It is the breadth and depth of your network, of your trusted relationships, that will define your success. So, make sure that you continue to build trusted relationships with a wide range of people from different walks of life and from different organisations. These relationships will be the most valuable thing that you can take with you in your career.

CHAPTER 6: GETTING TO KNOW YOUR CLIENT

You can only be an effective consultant if you try to understand your client. It's impossible to build trust if you don't attempt to understand the human elements of your client. All clients are different, but there are some basic questions you should always seek out the answers to:

- Who is your client? What do they do?
- What motivates your client?
- What is your client's role in the decision-making process?
- What is the business context in which your client operates?
- What are your client's goals?
- What are your client's fears and concerns?
- Who are your client's internal and external stakeholders?
- What do these stakeholders need from your client?
- What are your client's longer term career ambitions?
- What is their personal situation? What are their interests?

Finding answers to these questions will help you understand what makes your client tick. It will also give you insights into how to best approach and communicate with them. Remember, you are trying establish a sincere relationship of trust so that your client feels comfortable to open up and share their true needs.

So how do you find out this information? You can start by doing some research on your client's company, industry, and position.

You can also ask your client directly for this information. But be warned, not all clients will be forthcoming before they get to know you. In these cases, you'll have to read between the lines and use your intuition to fill in the gaps.

The best way to get to know your client is to spend time with them. This could mean having lunch or coffee together, going to meetings or events together, or simply spending time chatting in person or over the phone. The more time you spend with your client, the more likely they are to open up and trust you. It isn't the answers to the questions above that builds trust - it's the process you go through which demonstrates your sincere interest that creates trust.

Keep in mind that it's important to get to know your client as a person, not just as a decision maker. Learning about your client's personal life will give you insights into what motivates them and how to best communicate with them.

Finally, remember that it takes time to get to know someone. Don't expect to become best friends overnight. Just take your time, be patient, and be genuine in your interest in getting to know your client. With time and effort, you'll develop a trusting relationship that will serve both you and your client well.

You can learn a lot about your client before you even meet them through your network. Similarly, your client's network is full of people who can give you insights into what they're like, what they care about and how best to approach them.

Start by speaking to your mutual friends, colleagues or business contacts. Ask them for their thoughts on your client and what they think you should know about the person you are about to meet.

You can also do some online research. Social media can be a great way to get to know someone without even speaking to them. Have a look at their LinkedIn profile, Twitter feed or Facebook page to see what kind of things they're interested in.

Once you have built up a basic picture of you client, what do you do with the information?

First, use it to adjust your communication style. If you know that your client is shy, for example, you'll need to be more patient and take things at a slower pace.

Second, use the information to decide what sort of approach to take. If your client is very analytical, for example, you'll need to make sure that your thoughts and ideas are well thought out and backed up by data.

Ask the right questions. This means more than just asking their name and what they do for a living. You need to probe deeper in order to really understand who they are and what they want. Once you have asked these questions, it is important to listen carefully to the answers. Pay attention to both what the client says and how they say it. This will give you valuable insights into their true needs.

Use what you've learned to build trust. Remember that trust is built on shared values and common experiences. So if you can find ways to connect with your client on a personal level, you're more likely to develop a trusting relationship. Keep these things in mind as you get to know your client, and you'll be on your way to developing a strong, trust-based relationship.

Through your initial discussions and research, you are very likely to find commonality between you and your client. Commonality builds rapport, and rapport is the seed of trust.

When you find things that you have in common with your client, make sure to mention them. This could be something as simple as sharing a love of books or movies, or something more significant like having children the same age.

Commonality is the key to building trust, so use it to your

advantage as you get to know your client.

Once you feel rapport is being built, you can dig deeper and start to ask them about their own objectives. This could be their objectives for the project, their career objectives or even their personal life goals.

Asking about objectives shows that you are interested in them as a person, not just as a client. It also helps you to understand what motivates them and what they care about. This information will be invaluable as you work together.

Finally, don't forget to keep your own objectives in mind as you get to know your client. Remember why you're doing this in the first place – to serve your client and achieve the best possible outcome for both of you.

If you are in a position to help your client with their personal agenda, then the human connection - the essence of a relationship - will significantly improve.

You should also take the opportunity to learn about your client's business. You do not need to give the impression that you have answers to the many issues and complexities that they are likely to be involved with. Indeed, jumping to half-baked solutions can have the opposite impact of what you are trying to achieve.

You are not trying to find answers in these discussions, you haven't yet reached the depth of understanding to be able to. What you are looking to do is understand how their environment works; what the issues, challenges and opportunities are. Once you have this understanding, you can start to build a picture of where your client's business and life is going and how you can help them get there. You want to go on a journey of discovery.

As well as your client's objectives, you could also ask about their stakeholders objectives. Asking about stakeholders' objectives will help you to understand their interests and concerns. This information will be invaluable as you work together to deliver a successful outcome.

One thing to avoid is a transactional feel to these discussions. You will need to earn the right to delve into someone's business and personal life. But there is one key that will usually lead to your client being open and sharing answers to all of these questions. The key is the client seeing that openness from you.

Be open about your own objectives, purposes and experiences. In other words, share something of yourself. It is in the sharing that we gain trust. So if you want to build trust with your client, start by being open with them. Make sharing mutual and equal.

CHAPTER 7: THE RELATIONSHIP CONTRACT

When a new potential client meets you for the first time, they will make all sorts of assumptions about who you are and why you are there. It is your job to manage those assumptions, by showing that you really want to learn about them and their needs.

The underlying tone of the first few minutes of your first meeting will begin the process of creating the "relationship contract". It is important to get the tone right from the start. Formality breeds barriers, and fear of the meeting will create a lack of confidence. The relationship contract you want to create is one of openness and trust.

A lot of consultants go into the first meeting and worry about whether they will succeed in demonstrating their value. To overcome this, they wrongly attempt to impress with their intelligence, their expertise and instead they leave a scent of arrogance and formality. Luckily for you, those consultants won't be remembered as individuals - they'll be remembered as a faint voice of the firm they represent as they hide behind the brand and credentials of their organisation.

Be the opposite - be humble, let your clients feel like they are in the driving seat. This is not a battle of egos, it's about finding out whether you can help each other.

In a subtle way, make sure they know early on that you are not in the room trying to leave with a "win". They should get the feeling that this conversation is the beginning of a journey and there are no expectations or feelings of entitlement. If you can make them feel this way, they will open up to you and be much more likely to work with you in the future. The conversation should be fun and easy. You should both be energised by the discussion if the tone has been set right - if it feels like a chore, its a warning that you need to go back a few steps and reset the relationship contract.

Consultants often worry that if they cannot demonstrate their expertise in abundance, then they won't stand out and won't get any work from the relationship. They worry that they will only have nice conversations that never yield any further value. They worry about this because they don't understand that their expertise is taken for granted or that there credentials can be assessed later- what isn't taken for granted is human connection and trust.

With the relationship contract in place, clients often feel secure and empowered to ask you questions about what you do and your expertise without feeling exposed or compelled to "buy". Putting your client into this zone of comfort is a huge step forward and tends to result in a real exploration of the value you can offer. This is the best outcome you can achieve - a real interest in exploring your areas of expertise, your firm, your wider value and your client wanting to identify a fit between their needs and your services.

Your client is much more likely to want to meet you again and build a relationship if they don't feel like they're using up their goodwill credits with you when they ask you questions. It should be clear from your conversations that there are no expectations from you, and this will help them to feel like they can reach out to you without being worried that they're taking advantage of your good nature.

When they reach the point where they do need your help to find a solution, they will naturally reach out to you if the following three conditions are met.

> 1. The first condition is that they are able to make a mental connection between their issue and your potential ability to help (note the use of the word "potential").
>
> 2. The second condition is that you are accessible to their mind at a time when you may not be visible to them (being front of mind).
>
> 3. The third condition is that they do not feel uncomfortable reaching out - that they dont feel like they "owe" you for your time, your ideas, your audience or access to your network.

You have had control over all of these conditions through the conversations and interactions you've had to date.

Let's explore the first condition. The client needs to be able to connect their issue to your ability to help. Your ability to help is probably broader than you realise. The client may have a specific technical question - and they will have access to plenty of advisors who could help them with that question. There is usually a wider context or situation in which their question is set - and this is where you are more likely to be able to offer real value. The client may not see the connection - but if you have been paying attention, then you will have a good idea of what they are dealing with and how your skills and experience can be applied. You may also be able to help with your networks (if the client knows you have them) or by using the other experts in your firm.

The second condition is that you are accessible to their mind at a time when they need you. This requires that you are front of mind for them and easy to find. You become front of mind by being genuinely interested in them and their situation, by providing useful information without selling, by connecting with them on a human level and by being responsive when they reach out to you.

The third condition is that the client does not feel uncomfortable reaching out to you. This is where the relationship really starts to pay off for both of you. If the client feels like they "owe" you something, it puts a barrier between you and them that can be very difficult to overcome. The best way to avoid this is to make sure that all of your interactions up to this point have been about helping them, without any expectation of anything in return. If you have been helpful and responsive without selling or asking for anything, they will not feel like they owe you anything and they will be much more likely to reach out when they need help. If they feel like they are bothering you or taking up your time, they will not reach out. You need to give them the space to reach out on their own terms.

So how would you respond if during a conversation, it is clear that the client may have an issue. Should you wait to be asked, or do you proactively and energetically offer to help? The surprising answer is neither. I'm not saying that you should not offer to help them with a specific piece of work. The approach of your response should naturally go through the following three stages: **Empathy, understanding and support.**

First, you want to show that you understand and feel what they are dealing with. Second, you want to make sure that you understand the situation and what they are trying to achieve. Only then should you offer your help. This approach is much more likely to result in the client accepting your help, because it shows that you care about them and their situation, and that you understand what they are trying to achieve. The offer of support should not feel transactional, and you shouldn't let your feelings of "winning" a piece of work overshadow the emotional feeling that the client might have with the difficult issues that they are facing. Empathise with the client's response too. They might feel relieved or remain anxious. They might seem grateful or they might feel like they're doing you a favour. Recognise this response and respond accordingly. Save your happy feelings about your win until you get back to your office.

It is absolutely critical that you don't get frustrated about not being given work when you think it's obvious that you can do something for them. What seems like the right answer to you may well not feel like the right answer to the client and actually may not be the right answer depending on the capability of the client and the maturity of the situation.

For those of you that have been an adviser for a while, you are probably thinking that this is all well and good, but there are short-term pressures for your business and an expectation to succeed linked directly to your promotion chances. The answer to this is to increase the number of deep relationships that you have rather than turning into a short-term salesman. I have seen many consultants under pressure give into the temptation to short cut the relationship process and sell. They may well have some small successes at selling some products usually at an undervalued price. However, in the medium to long-term that relationship is destroyed and the financial performance of the individual and the firm is negatively damaged as a result of giving in to this temptation.

Of course, you can't just sit back and do nothing. You need to have an active strategy for deepening the relationships that you have. This means going beyond the basics of having a cup of coffee with your clients or taking them to lunch. It requires you to think about what they are trying to achieve in their business and how you can help them get there. Once you have a clear understanding of what they are trying to achieve, only then should you start thinking about how your firm's products and services can help them get there. If you lead with what your firm does rather than with what your client is trying to achieve, you will never build a deep relationship because the client will always see you as a vendor rather than as a trusted advisor.

The best way to deepen a relationship is by providing value to the client without expecting anything in return. This means really understanding their business and their industry and being able to provide insights that help them make better decisions. It also means being there for them when things are tough and they need a sounding board or someone to help them think through a difficult problem. And, it means being honest with them even when it might be difficult to do so.

Building deep relationships takes time, but it is time well spent. Not only will you be more successful in getting work from existing clients, but you will also find it easier to win new clients because your reputation as a trusted advisor will precede you.

This strategy pays off, and you will know that it has paid of when a really important issue for the client comes up and they call you. Really important issues typically create large amounts of tangible and intangible value - monetary and emotional. They also have an element of risk and often need to be resolved quickly. These are the times when clients need a trusted advisor, not a vendor. If you've been following the advice in this book, you will be that trusted advisor.

When you get that call, your first reaction might be one of excitement because you know that this is an opportunity to show how much value you can add. But resist that temptation! The client is already under a lot of stress and if you come across as too eager it will only add to their stress because they will feel isolated in their emotions. Instead, take a deep breath and focus on being calm and collected. This is not the time to think about how much this project might be worth or how it will help your career.

Another thing that trips up advisors that are trying to form a relationship, is entangling their specialism with their trusted advisor role. It is comfortable, and in fact very easy, to start talking in detail about something that you are very familiar with. However, if you want to create a trusted advisor relationship with someone, then you have got to give them the space to explore what it is that they need to do. This doesn't mean that you shouldn't share your ideas and knowledge - in fact its vital that you do - but make sure that you frame it as part of a discussion rather than trying to take charge and tell them what they need to do.

If you go into a meeting and say, for example, "I'm a qualified corporate tax adviser" as your opening statement because it is comfortable, you have already labelled yourself as a technical specialist and not their future trusted adviser. You have not aligned your purpose here with the image you are giving to the client. Your specialism, although comfortable, is almost a distraction and can pigeonhole you as a provider of a specialist service. Your role here is not this. It is a trusted advisor and a partner.

CHAPTER 8: SELL THE RELATIONSHIP, NOT THE PRODUCT

We have talked about why it is important to be a trusted advisor and not a salesman. In this chapter we'll explore this a little further.

Quite simply, it comes down to whether you want to add value to your clients by helping them to solve their problems or by providing a product. There may well be products that sit behind the value you can add as an advisor, there may even be products or specific services that your firm explicitly asks you to sell (or "cross-sell"). However, you should always focus on solving problems, because products can be commoditised, and commodities are more susceptible to pricing pressure.

If you want to be a trusted advisor, you need to get to the heart of your clients' problems. This means understanding their businesses and their industries. It's not enough to provide a product or service - you need to understand how it will benefit your clients, and how it will fit into their wider business strategies.

This is why being a trusted advisor is so important - because it's about providing value that goes beyond the product or service itself. It's about becoming an integral part of your client's business, and helping them to solve problems that they may not even be aware of yet.

You can sell a product to a client once, and in the best case, the product (or product-like service) might generate annuity income. However, a product is always going to be a commodity unless it is unique to you or your firm. As a consultant it is unlikely that you'll be able to offer a product that the clients sees as unique in itself. The thing that will make it unique is your involvement or the personal credibility that you put on the line by referring it to your client. At that point the value that your client is really receiving is based on the trust that you have between each other.

A commoditised product or service will always be susceptible to price pressure. You never want to be in the position that all of your hard work comes down to the price of your service. It shouldn't. You and your firm are providing complex and bespoke services.

No doubt you will be very familiar with the pitching process. When you enter a pitch process, you need to be able to be sure that the client doesn't see the service that you are offering as a commodity. It should feel unique. It should be about the trust that the client has in both the outcome, and in the people that are going to achieve the outcome for them. This is why you have spent time and energy creating a trusted relationship - because now - the client's choice will come down to trust.

You might also believe that there may be some exceptions to this, where a company or a government procurement processes require an arms-length tendering process and a balanced scorecard to be completed. But your should realise that even under these circumstances, your client will influence the process and influence the scorecard to achieve an outcome that they personally believe is the right outcome. In circumstances where a procurement process isn't a certainty, your relationship may have prevented a tender process from happening because you have spent time demonstrating the value they will get from you, rather than from just the product of the service. The benefit of this is clear. Both you and the client save a lot of time and cost by avoiding an unnecessary procurement process.

If you're a consultant at an advisory firm in any field, the reality is that you will have services or products that can be sold. And these products and services are apparently valuable. They create value or solve certain types of problems. Best of all, you are the expert and you are very familiar with how they work! There are two ways to take these products and services to a new client.

> Option 1: You can give your client a menu of services, or offer specific solutions when you get a sense that they might benefit from a service. You'd usually be doing this on a generic level and in a product orientated way because you don't know your client's issues enough to be able to tailor the solutions to their specific problems and their specific priorities.

> Option 2: Understand their priorities in detail first - well before you mention a service or a solution. Understand your client's individual priorities and their business priorities so that you are able to create a bespoke solution to fit the inevitable complexities of their situation. Once you have taken time to do this and to understand what the client's priorities are, then you will be in a much better place to figure out how to tailor your solutions and services so they can be assured that you are solving their specific issues - not a generic issue.

The financial consequence of taking "Option 2", is that a client would be willing to pay full value for a solution that solves their specific priorities from an advisor that they trust. Compare this to a solution that mostly solves an issue, or solves a problem that isn't high up on their agenda.

The personal consequence of taking "Option 2" is that your own relationship will be strengthened because you are able to filter out the products and services which don't really matter to them at that point in time. In addition, because you have taken time to understand your client's specific issue and their stakeholder's priorities, you can help them with value beyond the delivery of the service. You can now partner with them to articulate the value and the outcome to their boss and other stakeholders. You are now being given access and a voice to other important parts of the organisation. Your client's reliance on you, and their trust in you will be magnified many time during this process. This is one way that you know you have started to become a trusted advisor.

When a client does accept a service from your firm, it should only be part of the journey. It should enable you to use the opportunity to begin co-creating a vision of "what good looks like" with your client. The great thing about creating this vision, is that, over time and with patience, it usually leads to more services to be provided to fulfil the vision to its full potential.

On the flip side, if you take "Option 1", you are more likely to get short term business with less opportunity for repeat or referral business. The client may also be much less likely to see you as a trusted advisor and someone who is interested in solving their specific problems. Taking the time to understand your client's specific priorities and issues pays off in the long run - both financially and in terms of building a strong relationship founded on trust.

You will have seen Option 1 in action - a consultant might go to a client and say something like "We have developed a new service, it can save you £10 million pounds" or "there has been a change in regulation, and we know that companies like yours need a solution…. and here it is…let's discuss how much you'd pay for it".

They might manage to sell the product (usually of relatively low value) to the client. They client might even call them back because they want to talk about that product. But this is a transactional relationship rather than a trust-based relationship. The consultant is a salesman, not a trusted advisor.

Without that trust-based relationship they will struggle to remain relevant. They will also struggle to reach the top of the value chain because they don't understand the client or their business. The client will go elsewhere for the bigger priorities and the largest value will be found there.

Focus on the relationship, not on the product. Be a partner not a supplier or provider. If you are a a trusted partner, then you will have access to all of your client's issues, and you can be involved in solving them all. If your client needs some help with their strategy you can provide it. If they have a specific technical or regulatory problem - whatever it is you'll know about it and you'll be in a position to help.

Clients that value your relationship will also listen when you do have specific opportunities that you can take to them. They'll be open to advice because they trust that you will take the right services at the right time at the right cost that will provide value for them in one way or the other. Importantly there will be lots of opportunity for regular contact. This regular contact is going to be the only way that you can continue to understand what their current priorities are, and it'll be the only way that you generate enough trust that they will call you whenever they need someone to solve one of their problems.

CHAPTER 9: UNDERSTAND YOUR CLIENT'S AGENDA

A consultant might typically go into a client meeting with an agenda. This agenda is based on what they would like to achieve. As we have discussed, talking to your own agenda doesn't achieve the best outcome. So why do consultants do this?

There are usually four reasons.

- Firstly, it is what they are used to doing. They have been trained to come up with a plan and then execute it.

- Secondly, they may not be aware of any other way to go about things.

- Thirdly, they may be worried that if they don't stick to their agenda, the meeting will become unfocused and unproductive.

- The fourth reason is that it is easy! It is much easier to prepare for a meeting and feel confident in a meeting if you are talking to your own agenda.

So how do you solve this problem? The key is to be aware of it and to make a conscious effort to avoid it. When you are preparing for a meeting, try to think about what the client's agenda might be. What are they hoping to achieve from the meeting? What problems are they trying to solve? What information do they need from you? Once you have a good understanding of the client's agenda, you can then prepare accordingly. In the meeting itself, make sure that you keep the focus on the client and their needs.

Listen carefully to what they are saying and ask questions to clarify things. Only bring up your own agenda items when it is absolutely necessary and make sure that you tie them in with the client's goals. By following these simple tips, you can make sure that your meetings are much more productive and that you are providing real value to your clients. This approach will also ensure that the meeting is focused and productive, and that everyone leaves happy!

It is easy to see how consultants fall into this trap if they don't make a conscious effort to shift the agenda away from themselves and toward their client. It is extremely easy to go into a meeting with an idea of the solution you might provide and say to the client something that sounds like: "Look at all the clever things that I have to talk about. Look at all the hot topics that I know about. Let's talk through these and see whether any of them matter to you".

This is the typical consultant's agenda and it is a lazy way to prepare for a meeting. These consultants are trying to take a shortcut and talk about what they think should be important to the client without asking the client what is important to them.

Another useful tip is to avoid getting bogged down in the details. It is easy to get caught up in discussing minutiae when what the client really needs is a high-level overview. Remember, the goal of the meeting is to solve the client's problems, not to show off how much you know!

Let's imagine walking into a sofa shop. A salesman comes up to you and says *"Hi. Based on your clothes, the car you were driving and the fact that it is the weekend, I have made some clever presumptions about what you need. You are in your mid thirties and therefore you'll probably have a family, a mortgage and therefore I think you need this midrange, child friendly sofa. I'm very certain this is exactly what you need even though I haven't asked you. It's an average sized sofa, and I have assumed that you are likely to be an average sort of person, so therefore this sofa must be perfect for you. By the way, I'm so desperate to hit my targets, that if you buy the sofa from me today and make me look good in front of my boss then I will give you a discount".*

The last bit might actually be accurate, but the rest of it just wouldn't happen! No one needs an average sofa because no one is average. Plus, no one wants to be told what they need because they rightly believe they are in the best position to figure that out for themselves (albeit with a bit of direction).

The same is true in business. Clients don't want you to make assumptions about what they need and try to sell them a pre-packaged solution. They want you to take the time to understand their specific situation and then work with them to find the best possible solution.

The problem is that this scenario happens all the time with consultants. It is an everyday occurrence. The number of consultants I see walking into prospect meeting saying " I know other companies that are somewhat similar to your company. These are the things that you should care about and therefore here is a list of things that you need to do (implying that if they don't do it, then they are in the wrong). Obviously, consultants don't use these words explicitly, but this is in essence what they say far too many times. Feedback on professional services firms usually says something like "smart, but arrogant", and they are, and this is why.

The reality is that clients want you to listen to them, and then help them figure out what they need to do. This is a subtle difference, but an important one. So often consultants go into meetings with their own agendas and try to sell the client on what they think the client needs. This is a recipe for mediocrity.

I won't forget a client of mine talking to me about some of her other advisors, and saying:

> *"Why do consultants always come in and tell me how I should be running my business. I've been working my business for over a decade. I know the politics, I know the business, I know the financials, I know our HR objectives, I know my investors, I know my stakeholders. I run this business 12 hours a day 5 days a week every week and have done for over 10 years. Why do consultants you have never met before think that they know how to improve my business better than I do without even asking me what I'm trying to achieve?"*

I couldn't agree more. So often, consultants go into a meeting with the attitude that they know what's best for the client and try to sell them on their own agenda. If you want to be successful in consulting, you need to focus on the client and their needs, not your own agenda. Only by understanding the client's specific situation can you hope to find the best possible solution for them. Anything less is simply selling them a pre-packaged solution that may or may not be relevant to their situation.

The truth is your client will have their own agenda. You just need to spend time and a little bit of energy finding it first. It's hard work because its unknown and hard to prepare for. You really need to go into a meeting with the intention of learning about what they are trying to achieve, what their priorities are, and what their constraints are. Only then can you start to figure out how you might be able to help them.

To summarise, the next time you go into a meeting with a client, make sure you keep the following in mind:

1. The goal of the meeting is to solve the client's problems.

2. Listen to the client and try to understand their specific

situation.

3. Suppress your desire to sell them a pre-packaged solution.

4. Only by understanding their specific situation can you hope to find a solution that truly meets their needs.

CHAPTER 10: IT'S ABOUT GIVE AND TAKE

Balance is key in any relationship - personal or professional. In a professional relationship, your aim is both to add value using your own perspectives and to listen to your client's perspectives. Finding this balance (not necessarily in equal proportions) is key to maintaining and building the relationship. Give and take is critical.

Balance needs to be struck from the first conversation. That is getting the sequencing right in the discussion (which topics do you speak about first), getting the balance between talking and listening right, and getting the balance between being interested and being intrusive. You also need to strike the right balance in terms of the level of detail that you share. Too little information and you will come across as evasive.

The ability to find this balance is something that develops with time and experience. It is important to be aware of it as an ongoing process, not a one-off event.

Think about how you can ensure a balance between talking and listening. This is not always easy, as we can all be guilty of wanting to do too much of one or the other. One way to help with this is to make sure that you leave enough time for the other person to speak. If someone has been quiet for a while, then it may be worth creating space and inviting them through body language and open questioning to participate more openly in the conversation. Conversely, if someone seems to be doing most of the talking, then it may be worth gently steering the conversation back towards a two-way discussion.

The third balance to strike is between being interested and being intrusive. This can be a difficult one as you do not want to pry but, at the same time, you do want to be interested in the other person. A good way to find the middle ground here is to ask open questions that encourage the other person to share information with you. Recall from a previous chapter that sharing information about yourself can make the other person more open to sharing information about themselves.

Finally, think about the level of detail that you are sharing. Again, this is something that takes practice to get right. Too little information and you will come across as evasive. Too much information and you will be overwhelming. The key is to find a happy medium where you are sharing enough information to be helpful but not so much that it becomes overwhelming.

All of these decisions will need to be made on a case-by-case basis as each relationship is different. The important thing is to be aware of the balances that you need to strike and to adjust your approach accordingly.

You will need to decide where to begin the conversation. Should this be about your client's business? Should it be about the persons industry? Should it be personal? The answer to this question may be led by underlying expectations depending on how the meeting was arranged. If you were introduced to talk about a certain topic then then there may be an expectation that at least some of the conversation is spent talking about that topic. Indeed, it is possible that you may need to arrange a second meeting to hit the broader agenda once you have earned that right. The important thing is that you get a sense for what the other person wants and needs from this conversation.

Let's make the assumption that your first meeting has been positioned as a general introduction and the agenda is open. In this case, be prepared to take a broad, unstructured and unassuming approach to the conversation. You want to set the scene by telling the person a little bit about you (remembering to find that balance between too much and too little information). You may want to start with some general questions about them and their business. Remember, the key here is to be interested without being intrusive.

Explore a wide range of topics, trying to find some natural linkage between the different areas you touch on. You want to come across as knowledgeable and insightful without seeming like you are trying to sell something. Once you have built up a rapport, you can start to probe a little deeper into areas of particular interest.

The aim of this meeting is not to close a deal or get an assignment but, rather, to establish a relationship. As such, do not be afraid to give as well as take. If the other person seems open to it, offer some advice or insights that may be helpful. This could be in the form of articles, books, websites or even introductions to other people who may be able to help them.

The important thing is that you are seen as someone who is interested in helping them, not just someone who is interested in selling to them.

Use open questions such as "What do you think about X?" or "How are you finding Y?". These will encourage the other person to share their thoughts and feelings with you without putting them on the spot.

When it comes to sharing information about yourself, remember to keep it relevant and interesting. Do not try to force a connection between what you are saying and what they are saying but, at the same time, do not be afraid to make a connection if one naturally exists. For example, if they are talking about a problem they are having with a project, you could talk about a similar problem you had and how you resolved it. The focus should be on empathy, not on the solution.

Be helpful without seeming like you are trying to take over or sell them something. If you can find that balance, then you will be well on your way to establishing a strong professional relationship.

So why are open questions a good way to have great conversations? Open questions are good conversation starters because they encourage the other person to share information with you. Being open yourself is important because, as we mentioned before, sharing can make the other person more open to sharing themselves.

In addition, open questions help to create a more balanced conversation. If you are only asking closed questions, then the conversation will tend to be one-sided with you doing most of the talking. This is not only boring for the other person but it also gives them the impression that you are only interested in yourself.

Open questions help to create a more relaxed and informal atmosphere, which is important when trying to establish a rapport with someone. And, finally, open questions show that you are genuinely interested in the other person and their thoughts and feelings.

So next time you are having a conversation with someone, try to ask more open questions. You may be surprised at how much deeper and more interesting the conversation becomes.

At the end of the meeting, you want to leave the door open for further contact. This could be in the form of a follow-up meeting or simply an offer to keep in touch. Do not be too pushy here as you do not want to come across as needy or desperate. A simple statement that you enjoyed the conversation and would like to continue it at some point in the future should suffice.

This approach may seem a little slow and indirect but, trust me, it is worth taking the time to build up these relationships. The pay-off will come in the form of improved sales, better quality assignments and stronger referral business. Being proactive in your follow up will be important.

How much talking should you aim to do?

In general, you should aim to do less talking than the other person. The goal is not to dominate the conversation but, rather, to make the other person feel comfortable and engaged. The goal is to build a rapport with the other person, not to impress them with your life story.

It is important to avoid monopolising the conversation by talking about yourself too much.

If you find yourself doing most of the talking, then try to ask more open-ended questions. This will encourage the other person to share their thoughts and feelings with you, which will in turn make them more open to hearing what you have to say.

So what should you talk about?

The best topics of conversation are those that are relevant to the other person and their interests. This could be anything from their work to their hobbies or even their family. Find something that you have in common with the other person and then use that to start a conversation.

You can explore the other person's opinion on something, for example, current affairs or a recent movie. The important thing is that you are genuinely interested in their opinion. The content is less important here than the feeling.

Finally, it is always a good idea to have some light-hearted conversation up your sleeve. This could simply be sharing a funny but personal story. You can make the other person laugh and, at the same time, build a rapport with them.

Don't forget, the goal of all this is to build a rapport with the other person. So take your time, be genuine and, most importantly, be yourself.

Mirroring the depth of conversation that you would like to see is a very helpful tool to sub-consciously set the tone at that level. If you want the conversation to be light and friendly, be light and friendly. If you want to discuss the news or current affairs in more depth, raise those topics. If you want to understand something personal about the individual that you have to give them something personal about yourself. Similarly, if you want to understand the person's objectives then you might have to talk a little bit about what your own personal or business objectives are. Opening up, sharing and even showing some vulnerability is the basis of trust.

One tip - don't dive into controversial subjects unless you are absolutely sure that the other person is comfortable discussing them. These topics have a tendency to polarise people and you don't want to risk distancing yourself from someone else based on polarising opinions.

You can use your body language to create a rapport with someone. This could be matching their posture or mirroring their facial expressions. This will make the other person feel comfortable and, at the same time, show them that you are interested in what they have to say.

Your face, your eyes, and even your body need to show that you're interested. Nodding your head, tilting it to the side, and maintaining eye contact are all important non-verbal cues that show you're engaged in the conversation. You should also try to avoid crossing your arms or legs as this can make you appear closed off and uninterested. Instead, try to keep an open posture with your arms and legs uncrossed.

The best way to build a rapport with someone is to be genuine and authentic. So take your time, be yourself, and enjoy the conversation.

Active listening is an important way in which to have a sincere productive conversation. It requires your full attention to what the other person is saying. It means that you are not just hearing the words but taking in the meaning, the feeling and the message behind those words. You can demonstrate to the other person that you are actively listening by making eye contact, nodding your head, and giving verbal cues such as "uh-huh" and "yes" to show that you are following along.

Listening is key. In order to understand where a client is coming from, you need to be an active listener. This means being present in the conversation and not letting your mind wander. It also means hearing the words that are being said, and taking the time to process them before responding. If you can do this, you'll be able to build a better rapport with your clients and give them the attention they deserve.

Be aware of your own body language. Your posture, facial expressions, and hand gestures can all send a message, whether you mean them to or not. If you're crossing your arms or tapping your foot, for example, you may come across as impatient or uninterested. Paying attention to your own body language can help you project the right image and create a more positive impression.

It is also important to avoid interrupting the other person while they are speaking. This can be difficult, especially if you are eager to jump in and share your own opinion on the matter. However, it is important to resist the urge to interrupt and instead let the other person finish speaking. Once they are finished, then you can share your own thoughts on the matter.

Building a rapport with someone requires time and effort. However, it is well worth the investment as it can lead to better communication, deeper relationships, and a more enjoyable conversation. So take your time, be genuine, and enjoy the conversation.

If your client opens up about their concerns, you are being given permission to explore and dig deeper - to truly understand. If they have trusted you enough to talk about their issues, then you must acknowledge this and demonstrate that you care about those issues by asking more about them. Don't let your own discomfort from exploring further prevent your from doing this, as it will send the message that you're not interested in engaging in the discussion. You will have, in essence, turned down the invitation.

At this point, to avoid trying to solve their problems, you can turn the discussion into a coaching conversation. Coaching is all about helping the other person to find their own solutions. This is done by asking probing questions that help them to see the situation in a new light and come up with their own ideas for how to address the issue. Coaching is not about giving someone an answer. It's about helping them find their own answers.

So how do you explore answers a topic that you may not be familiar with yourself? When exploring a new topic with a client, it's important to be open and curious. This means that you need to ask questions and then listen carefully to the answers. Allow yourself to be a beginner in this exploration.

Be aware of your own assumptions and biases about the topic at hand and try not to let them influence the conversation. Instead, focus on what the other person is saying and let that guide the conversation.

Acknowledge what they are saying, and then ask probing questions to help them explore the issue further. These questions should be open-ended and should therefore not be seeking yes or no answers. Instead, they should start with words like "what", "how", and "tell me more about".

Some examples of probing questions that you could ask about a topic are:
- What is your biggest concern about this issue?
- What would be the ideal outcome of this situation?

- What steps have you already considered to address this issue?

- What resources do you need to solve this problem?

Don't feel scared to ask them to articulate their issues in detail. What are the consequences of the issue? What have they done about it so far? What are the possible next steps that they are currently considering?

If at any point during the conversation you feel like you are getting lost, or if the other person seems confused, it can be helpful to take a step back and summarise what has been said so far. This will help to ensure that everyone is on the same page and it will also help to move the conversation forward.

When asking probing questions, it is important to avoid sounding (or looking) judgmental or critical. Instead, focus on sounding curious and supportive. This will help the other person feel safe enough to share their thoughts and feelings with you.

Test the possible next steps that they have put forward and then help them to prioritise the ideas and decide what they're going to do next.

It is unlikely that you will get them to see this coaching conversation as a coaching conversation explicitly. However, they still need to buy in to the style of conversation. Honestly, it is a relatively easy and natural conversation to move into once they have been convinced that they are getting value from discussing the issue with someone else. They may already know this, or they may find this out by articulating their problems and explaining why it is a problem to you. Going on this journey with them of identifying the problem and understanding consequences that the problem can actually create urgency and the need for them to look to solve the problem more quickly.

It is very easy to accidentally move into passive listening. Passive listening is when you try to give the impression that you are listening, but in reality you are still focused on your own agenda, usually because you get distracted by your own thoughts, ideas or solutions. You might be thinking about the next thing you were going to say, you might be trying to take the conversation into a specific area that you want to talk about.

Either way it becomes very obvious very quickly that you are not really listening, that you're not focused on the issues that your client is facing, and as a consequence the conversation between you and your client is unlikely to be deep or authentic. They are unlikely to want to engage fully in your agenda as you are not engaging fully in their agenda.

One way to test how valuable a conversation has been is to say how you feel about the conversation. E.g. "I've really enjoyed this conversation, and found it very useful". This will help to ensure that the other person feels heard and it will also help to gauge how helpful the conversation has been for them. The tone and sincerity of response will also help you to understand how they felt about the conversation.

Giving and taking is a two-way street. In order to build a strong, productive relationship with a client, you need to be willing to give as well as take. This means being open to feedback, being responsive to requests, and being flexible when it comes to scheduling and other details. If you can do this, you'll be well on your way to developing a strong, lasting relationship with your clients.

CHAPTER 11: YOUR CLIENT'S PERSONALITY DOES MATTER

Personality matters. You need to be your authentic self, but it's undeniable that personal preferences and biases impact how clients want to hold a discussion. If you come on too strong, you may scare off a client who wants someone to listen more. Equally, if you're too passive, a client may feel like their concerns aren't being heard. There's a balance to be found, and it takes effort and attention to get it right.

You should base your style and content on your client's personality type. You need to give them what they need. If they want someone who will listen, be that person. If they want someone to be more assertive, then you need to be that person. It's all about giving them what they want and making sure that the communication is effective.

There are many different ways of classifying personalities, but for the purposes of this chapter, we will focus on the four personality types identified by the Myers-Briggs Type Indicator (MBTI). These are:

- Type A: analytical and logical

- Type B: easygoing and relaxed

- Type C: guarded and reserved

- Type D: emotional and expressive

Each personality type has its own strengths and weaknesses, and each will respond differently to different communication styles. It is important to be aware of your own communication style, as well as your client's personality type, in order to find a balance that works for both of you.

Type A personalities tend to be analytical and logical, and they prefer a communication style that is direct and to the point. They are often uncomfortable with small talk and prefer to get straight to the point. **Type A** personalities are very driven and competitive. They like to be in control and are often quite assertive.

Type B personalities tend to be easygoing and relaxed, and they prefer a communication style that is more informal and casual. They are often more comfortable with small talk and they like to build rapport before getting down to business. **Type B** personalities prefer to let others take the lead and aren't as concerned with being in control.

Type C personalities tend to be guarded and reserved, and they prefer a communication style that is more analytical and logical. They often need time to process information before they can make a decision, and they may not be comfortable with small talk.

Type D personalities tend to be emotional and expressive, and they prefer a communication style that is more emotional and expressive. They often need to feel a connection with their communication partner before they can open up, and they may not be comfortable with business talk.

When it comes to communication, there is no one-size-fits-all approach. You need to tailor the communication to the individual and make sure that it is effective. Pay attention to your client's personality type and give them what they want. It's all about finding a balance that works for both of you.

If you're not sure what type of personality your client has, try to observe their communication style and see what works best for them. If you can find a way to connect with them on a personal level, it will make the communication that much more effective.

Let's explore different personality styles that might clash and styles that work well together.

If you are Type A, you might find that Type D personalities are too emotional for your liking. You prefer to communicate in a more rational and logical way, while they may be more expressive and reactive. This doesn't mean that you can't work together, but it might take some effort to find common ground.

If you are Type B, you might find that Type A personalities are too driven and competitive for your liking. You prefer a more relaxed and easygoing communication style, while they may be more assertive.

If you are Type C, you might find that Type B personalities are too laid back for your liking. You prefer a more analytical and logical communication style, while they may be more easygoing.

If you are Type D, you might find that Type C personalities are too guarded for your liking. You prefer a more emotional and expressive communication style, while they may be more reserved.

It is really important to recognise that your clients will have different traits and different personalities. For example they may love detail or instead they might like big picture innovation. Your client might be risk averse or deliberative or they may make decisions based on their gut. They may be very direct in nature or they may come across very friendly. You must try to take some time in the early part of a relationship to understand what your clients personality is, and therefore what they need from you.

Some of my own clients at the beginning of my advisory career were technical in their approach. They did a technical job, had a technical education and tended to make technical decisions. They felt comfortable understanding detail and didn't take risk lightly. This profile contrasts with my own natural personality and with the personality of some of my other clients. For example other clients were very much future orientated, thinking about their businesses and their own careers 5 or 10 years into the future. They viewed things more strategically, trying to paint a vision and then execute on that vision rather than just implementing a specific project. They tended to get excited by new ideas and enjoyed creating loads of new ideas together with other people.

Clearly, these two types of individuals need very different things from their trusted advisor. Their trusted advisor needs to make them feel comfortable and needs to give them what they need. So if my client needed detail, they might have needed to understand the implementation plan over the next 12 months. They feel comfortable knowing that other people have gone through the same process, and so it doesn't feel like that they're taking a risk. In this situation I needed to take time collating the detailed plan, identifying a list of other clients have done similar projects, and giving them what they need in order to make a decision in a comfortable way.

On the other hand, giving detail and a 12 month plan to someone that wants to be spontaneous, and create a vision and a solution together would stifle their need for creativity and is likely to put structure place when that person doesn't want or even need structure. Recognising these differences and responding accordingly is critical to buildings a relationship where they feel comfortable with you.

Depending on the situation, your client may be under some stress. How might theses different personalities deal with stress differently?

Type A personalities tend to deal with stress by becoming more analytical and logical. They may become more task-oriented and less people-oriented.

Type B personalities tend to deal with stress by becoming more easygoing and relaxed. They may become more people-oriented and less task-oriented.

Type C personalities tend to deal with stress by becoming more guarded and reserved. They may become more task-oriented and less people-oriented.

Type D personalities tend to deal with stress by becoming more emotional and expressive. They may become more people-oriented and less task-oriented.

When it comes to stress, different personalities will react in different ways. It's important to understand how your communication partner is likely to react to stress, so that you can adjust your communication accordingly. If they are likely to become more analytical and logical, then you need to make sure that your communication is clear and concise. If they are likely to become more emotional and expressive, then you need to be prepared to listen and offer support. If they are likely to become more easygoing and relaxed, then you need to be prepared to take on more of the communication burden. And if they are likely to become more guarded and reserved, then you need to be prepared to give them space.

Different personalities will also have different needs when it comes to stress. Type A personalities may need more information and more details in order to feel comfortable. Type B personalities may need more reassurance and more support. Type C personalities may need more understanding and more empathy. And Type D personalities may need more space and more time.

Knowing your communication partner's personality type will help you to understand their needs and adjust your communication accordingly. This will ultimately lead to more effective communication and a better relationship.

You are also likely to need to put together a team, and to put different members of the team in front of your client. You will need to put the right people in front of the right clients at the right time.

- If you have a very analytical client, you will want to put your more detail-oriented team members in front of them.

- If you have a very creative client, you will want to put your more imaginative team members in front of them.

- If you have a very spontaneous client, you will want to put your more flexible team members in front of them.

- If you have a very guarded client, you will want to put your more reserved team members in front of them.

Different personalities will require different communication styles. Type A personalities tend to prefer direct and straightforward communication. Type B personalities tend to prefer more supportive and reassuring communication. Type C personalities tend to prefer more understanding and compassionate communication. And Type D personalities tend to prefer more distant and less personal communication. You will need to make sure your team knows this and can adapt to it as well. Your personal credibility extends to your team and others in your form or your network if you introduce them to your client.

You will be the one who is responsible for making sure that your team is working together effectively and that they are presenting a united front to the client. This means that you need to be able to manage different personalities and communication styles. It's not always easy, but it's important. If you can do it well, you will be an invaluable asset to any organisation.

So in summary, here are some key takeaways:

- Be aware of your own communication style and how it might impact your client.

- Be aware of your client's personality type and tailor the communication to them.

- Pay attention to how your client communicates and try to find a balance that works for both of you.

CHAPTER 12: BE PRESENT, BE RELEVANT

The frequency of your meetings and the environment in which you have your meetings are also important in determining how well your relationship evolves. If you only meet with your clients in-person once a year, it may be difficult to build rapport and trust. On the other hand, if you're meeting with clients too frequently, you may find it difficult to keep up the energy and interest. Choose a frequency that feels right for you and your relationship.

Another important factor in client relationships is the environment in which you have your meetings. If you're meeting in a busy coffee shop or restaurant, it may be difficult to have an intimate conversation. On the other hand, if you're meeting in a more formal setting, such as an office, it may be difficult to relax and build rapport. Choose an environment that feels comfortable for both of you and that will allow you to focus on your conversation.

So, regular catch ups, sometimes in an out-of-office setting are valuable. It's a good idea to schedule these in so that you can both plan for it and make the most of the meeting. You want to walk away from each meeting feeling like you've accomplished something, whether that's making progress on a project or simply getting to know each other better.

Most importantly, don't forget to have fun! If you're not enjoying your meetings, your clients probably aren't either. Find ways to make your meetings more enjoyable for both of you, and you'll find that your client relationships improve as a result.

Share your own thought leadership and share the thoughts of others that are relevant or interesting to your client. This kills two birds with one stone. Your client feels like they are getting useful information from you, while also seeing that you are on the cutting edge and doing your homework. This is a great way to add value and build rapport at the same time.

Be part of your clients' lives. If you know something big is happening in their personal life, such as a home move or the birth of a child, be sure to reach out and congratulate them. Similarly, if something major happens in your own life, don't hesitate to share it with your clients. This will help you build deeper relationships with them and they will appreciate feeling like they know you on a more personal level.

Enjoy your common interests with your client. If you have something in common with your client, such as a love of sports or a shared hobby, be sure to find ways to incorporate that into your meetings. This can be a great way to bond with your clients and make your meetings more enjoyable for both of you.

As the relationship becomes stronger, you may wish to introduce your clients into your personal or family network. This is a big step, but can really solidify the relationship if it's something that feels comfortable for both of you.

We've touched on the importance of meeting frequently when developing a strong relationship. This sounds obvious in many ways, but being front of mind and standing out from all the noise is key. Lots of other advisors will be talking to your client, and so your relationship and the trust that you are building with your clients will be the difference that shines through.

Clients want to know that you're available when they need you, but they also don't want to feel like they're bothering you all the time. Finding the right balance can be difficult, but it's important to try to be as responsive and not appearing like you are too busy to listen.

It is very easy to make excuses not to pick up the phone and call someone that you haven't spoken to for a couple of months. You might vaguely say that you'll call them, but get distracted and never get around to it. Sometimes you'll drop an email which may or may not get a response. In truth, especially when there is no agenda, some consultants are relieved when there is no response to an email, because they don't have to create time or a purpose for a meeting. Of course, the longer your leave it, the more comfortable it is not to get in contact. If you feel like this, your relationship isn't as strong as you might hope or believe.

When you have a good relationship with a client, regular communication is key to maintaining that relationship. If you go too long without talking to a client, they may forget who you are or what you do. Even if they don't forget about you, they may start working with someone else who is more involved.

The frequency of your communication will depend on the nature of your business and your relationship with the client. In general, though, it's best to err on the side of being too communicative rather than not communicative enough.

So how often should you be meeting with your clients? In general, a good aim is for at least once a quarter. This gives you enough time to stay in touch without being too intrusive. Of course, some clients will want to meet more often than that, and some will be fine with meeting less often. It all depends on the relationship and what works best for both parties.

If you're not sure how often to meet with your clients, just ask them. They'll be happy to let you know what works best for them. And if you're not sure how to bring up the topic, just say something like, "I want to make sure I'm giving you the best possible service. How often would you like to meet?"

Once you've established a meeting schedule, be sure to stick to it. If you consistently meet with your clients on a quarterly basis, they'll start to expect it. And if you suddenly stop meeting with them, they may think you don't care about them anymore.

When you make the effort to connect with your clients on a regular basis, it shows that you value their business and their relationship with you. It also gives you a chance to stay up-to-date on what's going on in their lives and their businesses. So don't be afraid to pick up the phone or send an email every now and then. Your clients will appreciate it.

At the start of this process, sometimes it is useful to have a structure to facilitate regular meetings with your relationships. You may agree to have quarterly catch ups. If this is the case then you can make sure that these go into the diary so that there is already a joint expectation that these regular meetings will play out they won't be forgotten. Eventually, the need for this structure will fall away because you will naturally find reasons to meet and talk on a regular basis.

Many consultants are very good at relationship building when they first meet someone. They will go out of their way to make a great first impression and ensure that the prospect feels comfortable and special. However, too often after the deal is won, those same consultants will go back to their old ways and start to take the client for granted. You need to work hard to maintain the same level of communication and service after the deal is done as you did before it was won.

Your clients are your best advocates. If you keep them happy, they'll sing your praises to anyone who will listen. Not only that, but they'll also be more likely to give you referrals, which can help you grow your business.

So if it's so easy, why don't consultants do this with all their clients? In some cases, it's because they fail to make a conscious link between what they are reading, or what they are doing with another client with their other client relationships. It is very easy to get into the habit of not thinking broadly and beyond what is right in front of you.

The reality is that there are numerous reasons to catch up. In most Industries, things change on a very regular basis, and picking up on their business' news and reacting to it is actually a very easy thing to do. It also shows that you care about what is going on in their lives. Furthermore, as a result of having that conversation you may find out about an opportunity, or a problem, which you can help with.

By far the best reason to catch up face to face is to share views or ideas about something that's going to be current to them. So this might be about trends that you're seeing outside of your clients industry but that is likely to affect them too. You don't need to have all the answers, in fact sometimes it's easier to have a fulfilling conversation if you don't have all the answers. It is enough to be interested and to be able to have a conversation and explore the issues. Being able to talk about things that are going on in their industry, or in the world, is a great way to build rapport with your clients. It shows that you're interested in what's going on in their lives and that you care about their business.

When you are talking about specific issues, it may feel comfortable to discuss what you think about the issues and how it affects you or your business. This is fine, but give them space to talk about how it affects them, and ask him directly what they think and what their views are. Show that you actually care about their views and then spend some time talking about those views and be open about whether you agree with them or disagree with them.

So to recap, the benefits of regular catch-ups with clients are that it shows you value their business and the relationship, it allows you to stay up to date with what's going on in their lives and businesses, and it gives you a chance to share your views or ideas about something that's current to them. So next time you're thinking about picking up the phone or sending an email, ask yourself if there's something you can chat with your client about that would be of interest to them. You might be surprised at how much they appreciate it.

CHAPTER 13: CREATE, GROW AND SHARE YOUR NETWORK

When it comes to your professional network, sharing is definitely power. By sharing your network with your clients, you can create opportunities for them that they may not have otherwise had.

Your network provides you with a huge amount of value. It brings you clients, it encompasses all of your relationships, it values your expertise, ideas and solutions. Most importantly, it carries your brand, your professional identity. We'll talk more about brand later.

Sharing your network with your clients not only opens up opportunities for them, but it also creates trust and builds relationships. Your clients will see that you're not just interested in making money, but that you genuinely care about their success. And when your clients succeed, you succeed. It's a win-win situation.

By sharing your network with your clients, you show that you're invested in their success. This can build trust and strengthen your relationship. So, if you're looking to create opportunities for your clients and build strong relationships, don't be afraid to share your professional network.

The key to success is to think of your clients not as only people who purchase your services, but as individuals with their own networks and relationships. When you start to see them this way, the opportunities for introducing them to other contacts and colleagues become endless.

This chapter focuses on creating your network, using it effectively and growing it quickly but authentically. If you have yet to develop your professional network, start with these tips:

Be generous: Give before you receive. By giving, you create goodwill and build trust. When you're generous with your time, advice and resources, people are more likely to be generous with you.

Be authentic: Be yourself and don't try to be someone you're not. People can see through inauthenticity, so it's important to be genuine in all your interactions.

Be helpful: Offer help without expecting anything in return. When you're helpful, people are more likely to want to help you. And when they do need help, they'll remember that you were there for them and they'll be more likely to return the favor.

Be a good listener: Listen more than you talk. By really listening to people, you can learn about their needs and how you can help them. People will also appreciate that you're interested in what they have to say.

You've already got a huge network. Even if you're just starting your career, you have spent 20 years building it. Your network has been built on friendship, trust, commonality and this isn't going to change one bit. In fact the secret is not to let it change. The mistake many people make when they start their business is that they forget about their personal network and only focus on building a new professional one. Don't! Your personal network is your most valuable asset.

Yes, of course you should also build a new professional network but don't forget about the people who have known you since you were born, the ones who have seen you through thick and thin. These are the people who will always be there for you, no matter what. These are the people who will champion you and your business. These are the people who will be your biggest fans. So never underestimate the power of your personal network. It is invaluable.

Now let's look at how you can use your professional network to create opportunities for your clients.

First, consider who in your network could help your client. Maybe you know someone who can provide them with advice, or introduce them to someone they need to meet. Perhaps you have a connection at their dream company. Whatever it is, see how you can use your network to benefit your client.

Next, reach out to your contacts and ask for their help. This can be done in person, by email or even over social media. Let them know what you're trying to achieve and how they can help. Be specific in your request and be sure to thank them in advance for their help.

Finally, follow up with your contact after they've helped your client. Thank them again for their help and let them know how much it was appreciated. This will help to build a strong relationship and they'll be more likely to help you again in the future.

So how do you begin building your professional network?

Start by attending industry events and networking functions. These are great places to meet new people and start building relationships. You can also connect with people online, through social media or professional networking sites.

When you're meeting new people, take the time to get to know them. Find out about their work, their interests and what they're looking for in a network connection. Then see how you can help them. Maybe you know someone who can help with their job search or you have an idea for a project they're working on.

Whatever it is, offer your assistance.

Look for people that operate in similar areas of work, for example colleagues within your organisation but perhaps with different skill sets and specialisms. It is often these people that can be the most useful when it comes to networking, as you can share information, advice and resources.

Next, look at extending your network to those inside your organisation that work in different fields but are likely to advise similar clients. This type of network will be essential in referring you to their clients, and they are easy to connect with and get to know on a personal level.

You should also look for like minded professionals in complementary fields in other organisations. These people are perfect for cross-referrals and can provide you with a wealth of knowledge and experience. They will also be talking to your current and prospective clients. When they talk about you, they provide you with enhanced credibility.

Once you have a network of professionals that you trust, you can introduce them to your own clients and colleagues. By doing this, you are providing your clients with access to a wealth of knowledge and experience that they may not have otherwise had. You are also increasing your own exposure and credibility.

Do not hoard your network - many people do because they are scared to share. But by doing this, they are only depriving their clients of the opportunity to benefit from it. What they are really doing is limiting the value of their network to themselves.

So, actively share your network with others. Create a network between your clients. The benefits are huge. It will make you and your network more successful. Your clients will refer you to their contacts and vice versa. You will have a larger, more diverse network as a result which can only be beneficial to everyone involved.

Your network is extremely valuable, but there is one thing that is more valuable than your network of people. That is those same people connected to each other. A connected network is a powerful thing.

When you introduce two people who share common goals, they can help each other achieve those goals. They can also open up new opportunities for each other that they may not have otherwise had access to.

If you have a contact who is looking for a new supplier, you can introduce them to one of your contacts who provides that service. But if you also introduce your client to other contacts who may be interested in that service, they will have a whole network of potential customers.

A connected network is more than the sum of its parts. It is a powerful tool that can be used to achieve common goals.

By being connected to lots of individuals you are able to interact and add value to all of those individuals. By connecting your your network up with each other, they are able to access value that you might not be able to provide by leveraging the rest of your network.

It is very common for consultants to feel like they are less valuable when they are cut out as the go-between between the relationships. However, in reality this is not true at all. If your client speaks directly to another colleague or contact of yours and they are able to get value, not only will they know that you introduced them, but they will also know that you trust them enough not to gate access.

Furthermore, you have provided two people within your network with commonality. This commonality is yourself, and as a consequence there likely to talk about you when they have conversations and you're not there. Given that these are likely to be positive conversations, the trust that both of these individuals have in you will be enforced by the experiences that the other has had of you as well. As a consequence, by connecting your relationships together you are in fact the strengthening the relationships that you have with everyone that you connect.

Chances are you have already created friends in your personal life by linking groups of friends with other friends. This feels quite natural, and you as an individual benefit from having a closely linked up network of friends and family. The same is true when applied to your professional life.

Let's think about the value of connecting your colleagues to each other. Lots of consultants operate in their technical silos. They are good at introversion and product development when ideas come from the inside. They are less good at creating out-of-the-box ideas because to do this you need to collaborate with external advisors. The game-changing ideas usually come from taking ideas that exist outside of an ecosystem, and internalising them within a new ecosystem.

If you have a network of colleagues, and they are connected to each other, then they can share ideas with each other. These ideas may be things that they have seen in other organisations, or it may be new ways of thinking about problems that they have come across. By sharing these ideas with each other, they are able to create new solutions to problems that they may not have been able to solve before.

It is also worth noting that when you connect two colleagues who share common goals, they are likely to help each other achieve those goals, share ideas and create new and valuable propositions - they can innovate!

Connecting clients to each other can also be extremely valuable to you and your firm. It is likely that they will share similar issues. If you're helping one client solve an issue, then it is likely that other clients have the same issue. If they're connected, more clients are likely to come to you for help, even if you haven't explicitly told each one that you can help.

So go ahead and start sharing your professional network with your clients today. You'll be surprised at the doors that open up for them - and for you.

CHAPTER 14: BE OPEN, BE PERSONAL, BE A FRIEND

When it comes to personal relationships, we all understand the importance of trust. Well, it's no different in business relationships. The key to any relationship is communication and transparency.

Why do personal relationships and professional relationships feel so different? For one, we communicate differently at work. We often use formal language and we're usually talking about business-related topics. But the biggest difference is that we don't always get to know our clients on a personal level.

So how can you turn your professional relationships into personal relationships? It's actually quite simple: by making the **effort** to get to know your clients on a more personal level. Here are a few tips:

1. Talk about things other than work

When you're talking to a client, try to steer the conversation towards non-work related topics. Find out what they like to do in their free time, what their hobbies are, etc.

2. Spend time together outside of work

Hanging out with someone outside of work is a great way to get to know them on a more personal level. You can grab lunch together, go for coffee, or even just take a walk.

3. Drop the formality in your conversations.

When you're talking to a client, try to use more casual language. This will help to make the conversation feel more personal and friendly.

4. Show your personality

Don't be afraid to show your personality to your clients. Let people see who you are outside of your professional persona.

By making an effort to get to know the clients you work with on a more personal level, you'll find that your relationships will improve both professionally and personally. Just remember to be respectful of people's personal space and boundaries, and to take things slowly. After all, relationships of any kind take time to develop.

You shouldn't be afraid of sharing things about you or your family, in the same way that you would with your friends. Human beings naturally respond to someone opening up to them and showing trust by opening up themselves. And it is the information that you get from these conversation that will be most valuable in the long-term.

Sharing commonalities is a great way to start building trust with someone. It could be as simple as both of you liking the same sports team or movie, or having children the same age. But it doesn't stop there. You can also share your values and beliefs. This is what will really help you to connect with someone on a deeper level.

Of course, it's important to remember that not everyone is going to want to open up to you right away. And that's perfectly okay. Just take things slowly and be patient. The more effort you put into getting to know someone, the more likely they are to reciprocate.

Over time, the strongest client relationships develop into friendships. You know you have reached this position when it doesn't feel strange inviting your clients over for dinner at your house. Clearly you don't want to start a relationship with family dinner invitations, but once you have reached this level of comfort with each other, it is a sign of a very successful professional relationship.

Having social meetings outside of work, possibly not even discussing work at all, strengthens the relationship significantly. This might be watching a football match after work, going out for lunch, or it might be asking them to get involved in a charity that you care deeply about. If a client says no a couple of times, it probably means that they are not ready for this stage of commitment yet so it's probably worth trying something a little less full on... maybe a coffee.

If you are the kind of person that likes equations, you can use the equation below to think about how to approach relationships in the right way:

Trust Based Relationship =

Intimacy + Credibility - Self-orientation

Let's break this equation up into its component parts:

Intimacy: Better trust based relationships are intimate. What does this mean? It means that the parties share information with each other. They're open and honest. When you develop a relationship with someone, there are usually 3 layers of intimacy:

1. Task-based: Can we complete the task at hand?
2. Personal: Do I like this person? Do they seem like a good person?

3. Private: What is going on in this person's life? What do they really think about something I care about?

Credibility: Credibility has to do with whether or not your client thinks you are competent. In other words, can you actually do what you say you can do? For example, if you tell me that you're an expert in search engine optimisation, but your website is nowhere to be found on Google, I'm going to have a hard time believing you.

Self-orientation: This last part of the equation is probably the most important, and it's also the one that most people struggle with the most. Self-orientation refers to whether or not you are focused on your own needs or the needs of your client. If you're always trying to sell me something, or if you're constantly talking about yourself, I'm going to have a hard time building my trust in you. On the other hand, if you're always trying to help me solve my problems and meet my needs, I'm going to trust you a lot more.

The bottom line is that trust is the foundation of any strong relationship, whether it's personal or professional. If you want to turn your professional relationships into personal relationships, you need to focus on building trust. The best way to do this is by being open and honest with your clients, demonstrating your competence, and always keeping their needs in mind.

Avoid arrogance in your conversations with your client. It is a significant destroyer of trust. Be transparent, be vulnerable, let your clients know that you're still learning and growing just like they are. You are not expected to know everything - indeed your client will be put off if you give the impression that you think you know best. You are not better than your client - you are complimentary to your client.

Your discussions should feel like a peer-to-peer discussion. You will fill in gaps that each other has - whether that's with context, outcomes, ideas, networks, subject matter expertise or experiences. You will complement each other through your discussions by creating a virtuous cycle of creating ideas and solutions. We've all been there - a great discussion gets an energy of its own.

Make plenty of eye contact (without staring). How does eye contact help? It builds trust. It makes you appear more confident and more credible. People who don't make eye contact can come across as shifty, untrustworthy, or even like they're hiding something. The same applies to smiling - use smiling to show them that are enjoying the conversation. Why does smiling help? Because when we see someone smile, it activates the same muscles in our own face, and that makes us feel happy. So not only does it make you appear more trustworthy, it also makes the other person feel good.

The key is to be genuine - if you're not a naturally smiley person, don't force it. The same goes for eye contact - if you're not comfortable making sustained eye contact, that's OK too. Just do your best to be open and honest, and let the relationship develop organically.

We all naturally use non-verbal gestures to indicate our engagement and understanding of the conversation that is taking place. It allows real time and transparent feedback of the discussion without disrupting the flow of the conversation. Non verbal cues can give away your real state of mind in the same way as verbal cues can. However, non-verbal cues are more difficult to control as they tend to show subconsciously.

As an example, after someone talks through something complex or convoluted, they may ask "does that all make sense". If you're not sure, you might say something like "ummm, I think so". Even though you think you are saying yes, your voice is giving a verbal cue to the contrary. Non-verbal cues can achieve the same thing. You may narrow your eyes, purse your lips or look away in thought, all of which are strong cues to the other person that you require to think it through or even that you disagree with what is being said.

These cues can be powerful and useful as long as you're aware you're doing it and its used in the right way. A poor non-verbal cue might be shaking your head or giving a disagreeing look before the other person has even finished what they are saying - this is tantamount to interrupting the other person verbally and saying "no, you're wrong" without letting them finish.

It is important to regulate your own engagement - enjoy the discussion, and focus on what your client is saying. If you find your mind starts drifting, try changing the energy level of the conversation. Get excited about the topic, or bring up a related story or experience. If you're both on the same wavelength, the conversation will flow naturally and easily.

Two further tips are: Be sincere and take a risk by giving your opinion.

Sincerity means being genuine in what you say and do. When we're talking to someone, we can usually tell if they're being sincere or not. If they seem like they're just going through the motions, or they're not really interested in what we're saying, it puts us off. On the other hand, if someone is genuinely interested in us and what we have to say, it makes us feel good. So when you're talking to your clients, make sure you're genuinely interested in them and what they have to say. Don't just go through the motions - be real, be genuine, be yourself.

Giving your opinion can be a risk - after all, you don't want to offend your client or put them off. But if you're sincere and genuine, it's more likely that they'll appreciate your honesty. And even if they don't agree with you, at least you're showing that you're not afraid to express your opinion.

The final point I want to make in this chapter is a plea. Please make a call or send a personal note rather than sending a formal email - especially in place of those copy and paste emails that you send out to everyone - its really obvious, and you're not making them feel like an individual but like one of many. If you can call, do. It's far more productive, far more engaging, and you are likely to achieve more in a single call than multiple emails.

CHAPTER 15: CREDIBILITY

In an earlier chapter, we touched on the importance of credibility when it comes to building trust. In this chapter, we'll go into more depth about what credibility is and how you can use it to build trust with your clients.

Credibility is the quality of being believable or trustworthy. When you're credible, people are more likely to believe what you say and trust you. I have purposefully left the topic of credibility towards the end of the book because by now you'll know that trying to build deep relationships by focusing purely on expertise won't work. However, credibility with your client is important, so we'll go into more detail now.

Perceived credibility can come from lots of sources. How you are face to face, what your social media profiles say about you, and what you get when someone does a Google search on you. Away from online, credibility also comes from what your colleagues, peers, and clients say about you, particularly when you're not in the room. It may even extend to what newspapers, trade press, or public interviews say about you.

Credibility is important, not least because a lack of credibility, especially in today's online environment can be damaging. Inconsistency can also significantly harm your credibility. For example, if your LinkedIn profile suggests you have expertise in a certain area, but your posts never refer to that area, people might start asking questions. At the very least it puts out there that you lack passion in the area in which you are an expert.

There are a few different ways to build credibility with your clients. One way is by demonstrating your expertise. Another way to build credibility is by being consistent in your actions and words. If your clients can rely on you to do what you say you're going to do, they'll be more likely to trust you.

Building trust with your clients is essential to a successful business relationship. By demonstrating your credibility, you can show your clients that they can rely on you, and that will make them more likely to trust you and do business with you.

There are a few different ways to build credibility:
- Demonstrate your expertise
- Be consistent in your actions and words
- Provide evidence to support your claims

You will naturally earn a level of credibility from your qualifications and from your association with your firm. You will also benefit from being referred in by another person. If you have a personal recommendation this will give you some extra kudos. But there are things that you can do yourself to increase the level of credibility in your relationship with clients:

Demonstrating your expertise is one way to build credibility with your clients. If you can show that you know what you're talking about, they'll be more likely to believe you and trust you. There are a few different ways that you can demonstrate your expertise:

- Write articles or blog posts on topics that your clients are interested in.

- Give presentations or webinars on topics that are relevant to your clients.

- Participate in discussions on forums or social media platforms where your clients are active.

- Publish research reports on topics that would be of interest to your clients.

Being consistent in your actions and words is another way to build credibility with your clients. If they see that they can rely on you to do what you say you're going to do, they'll be more likely to trust you. There are a few different ways that you can be consistent:

- Keep your promises;

- Be punctual;

- Respond to client queries promptly; and

- Follow through on your commitments

Providing evidence to support your claims is another way to build credibility with your clients. If you can back up what you're saying with data or research, your clients will be more likely to believe you and trust you. There are a few different ways that you can provide evidence:

- Cite studies or statistics that support your claims.

- Share case studies of previous clients who have benefited from working with you.

- Point to awards or recognition that you've received from your peers.

Building trust with your clients is essential to a successful business relationship. By demonstrating your credibility, you can show your clients that they can rely on you, and that will make them more likely to do business with you.

It is likely that you operate in a tighter circle than you think. This means that negative stories can damage you quickly but it also means that you can quickly become very credible if you do the right things.

How can your credibility with your clients be damaged?

- You make a promise and don't deliver.

- Your client sees you in a negative light e.g. being argumentative with someone in a meeting.

- Your client starts to feel that your priorities are not aligned with theirs e.g. you are trying to push them towards a product that they don't want.

- Your online presence is not up to date or is misleading in some way.

Don't suggest that you know things about things that you don't. It will be quickly exposed and you'll lose all credibility, not just with that client but also with others who hear about it. Ensure the quality of your work and the work of your team remains high. If it drops, so will your credibility.

Credibility can be built in many ways, but it's essential to remember that it takes time. You need to consistently demonstrate your expertise and your commitment to your clients to build trust with them. Once you have that trust, you'll have a strong foundation on which to build a successful business relationship.

CHAPTER 16: CREATIVE MEETINGS

When it comes to deepening relationships with clients, there are few things more valuable than having informal, free-flowing discussions. These types of conversations tend to be more authentic and allow for a deeper level of connection. I have always enjoyed and thrived in meetings with no fixed agenda. Indeed, I can sometimes struggle in meetings that are overly structured. In overly structured meetings, my energy levels drop and quality and delivery both suffer.

For others, they might thrive in structured situations, but an unstructured meeting can sap their energy. It is important to understand your preferences and those of the people you are meeting with. If there is a mismatch, it can lead to frustration on both sides.

But sometimes, despite having a preference for structure, you will need to become comfortable without it. This is especially true when meeting with clients. In many cases, they will not want or need a structured conversation. They might just want to chat about their business, their industry, or the latest news.

Some clients may need this type of meeting to operate at their best, and to be most engaged. You need to be able to give them what they need. So how can you make sure you are comfortable in an unstructured meeting?

Here are a few tips:

- First, it is important to understand that not all meetings need to be structured. It is perfectly fine to have some time without a specific agenda.

- Second, when you are in an unstructured meeting, it is important to be flexible and adaptable. The conversation might go in unexpected directions, and that is okay.

- Third, it is still important to be prepared for unstructured conversations.

- Finally, it is important to remember that unstructured meetings can be just as valuable as structured ones. They can allow for deeper conversations and greater connection. So if you are uncomfortable with them at first, don't worry, you will get used to them in time.

Of course, this can be challenging if you are used to having everything planned out in advance. But it is important to remember that these types of conversations are opportunities to deepen relationships and get to know your clients better. If you can learn to be comfortable without a fixed agenda, you will be able to make the most of these valuable opportunities.

I would like to bust a myth. Some people assume that advisors that are comfortable without structure are "winging" their meetings. This is not the case. The best way to be successful in an unstructured meeting is to prepare rigorously in advance. This means having a good understanding of the client's business, industry, and the latest news and developments relevant to them. Only then will you be able to truly thrive in an unstructured conversation.

So, how else can you prepare for meetings with no agenda?

- First, it is important to understand the client's business. What are their goals? What are their challenges? What is happening in their industry?

- Second, you should have a good understanding of the latest news and developments relevant to the client. This includes both industry news and general business news.

- Third, you should have a good understanding of the client's personality. What do they like to talk about? What makes them comfortable? What makes them uncomfortable?

- Fourth, you should have a good understanding of your own strengths and weaknesses. What do you do well? What do you struggle with? How can you best serve the client?

- Fifth, it is important to have a list of questions prepared in advance. This will help you keep the conversation flowing even when there are lulls.

- Sixth, it is important to be patient. In some cases, the conversation might not flow as smoothly as you would like. But if you are patient and let it take its natural course, it will eventually find its way.

- Finally, it is important to remember that not every meeting needs to have a specific purpose or goal. Sometimes, the best meetings are the ones where you simply allow the conversation to meander. These can be some of the most valuable opportunities to deepen your relationship with the client.

So, if you are feeling uncomfortable about having an agenda-less meeting with a client, don't worry. Just remember to prepare in advance, be flexible, and go with the flow.

Sometimes, when there is no agenda, you may worry about running out of things to talk about. If this happens to you, one method of coping with this is to quickly think of a topic related to the last question or issue discussed. For example, if the conversation lulls after discussing a client's business goals, you could ask about their plans for achieving those goals. If the conversation lulls after discussing industry news, you could ask the client for their thoughts on those latest developments.

One thing to bear in mind for these types of conversations is that you want to keep them as strategic as possible, and focused on outcomes. You want to deep-dive into their issues but from their perspective rather than a technical perspective. It is really useful to approach a discussion this way as you will demonstrate real engagement and at the same time, your client will have had the opportunity to clearly articulate their issue to someone else. It may be the first time that they have been given the space to spell it out. Clarifying their views in their own mind is the first step on the journey to creating - indeed co-creating - a solution. The benefits of solving the problem will also become more apparent to them, and probably more acute.

Don't be scared to spend a good chunk of time going through one issue. Taking your time, and iterating through a specific issue is a critical element of successful coaching. Remember, the goal is not to solve their problems in one sitting but rather to help them find clarity and develop a plan of action.

Avoid superficially covering lots of issues and avoid trying to squeeze a large number of items into a one-hour catchup. 10 minutes per item might feel efficient, but it's usually a waste of an hour. There will be no depth, no time for an engaged conversation where you can demonstrate real passion and understanding for the problem, no idea generation and no progress. You can easily exchange a longer list of issues by email or cover them by phone. Face-to-face meetings are an opportunity to dig, explore, understand and create. Not doing so is a huge mistake.

Other tips for coaching your client include:

1. Listen more than you talk. This is crucial. You want to create an environment where the client feels comfortable talking and sharing their thoughts and ideas. The only way to do this is to listen more than you talk.

2. In general, don't offer advice too quickly unless asked. It is tempting to want to offer solutions to the client's problems straight away. But resist the urge to do this unless the client specifically asks for your advice early.

3. Focus on the future. One of the goals of coaching is to help the client develop a plan for moving forward. So, it is important to keep the focus on the future rather than dwell on past mistakes or problems.

4. Help the client find their solutions. This is perhaps the most important goal of coaching. You want to help the client find their solutions rather than try to impose your own ideas on them.

5. Be supportive and positive. As a coach, it is important to be supportive and positive. This will help the client feel more confident and motivated to find solutions to their problems.

If you follow these tips, you will be well on your way to having successful coaching conversations with your clients.

To generate a creative conversation that focuses on outcomes, it is also helpful to get the client to articulate the consequences of not fixing the issue. This can help to surface some of their fears and motivators. Here are some questions you could ask to get the conversation started:

- What would happen if the issue is not addressed?

- What are the consequences of not fixing the problem?

- What are the risks associated with not taking action?

- What are the potential costs of not addressing the issue?

The great thing about asking about the consequences of not solving the issue is that it will get the client focused on solving them. Once the client is ready to focus on solutions, you can start to explore options and possible courses of action. You can then co-create the solution and ultimately become part of the solution.

This is where your creativity and lateral thinking will really come into play. It is important to come up with a range of possible solutions rather than fixating on one particular solution. This will help to ensure that you find the best possible solution for the client.

You will now have earned a fantastic and welcome opportunity to give your opinions on solutions. Share your ideas and thoughts freely on the issue. You can use a range of experiences to do this. Create analogies with other industry trends. Talk about what you are seeing at your client's competitors and peers.

Deep diving into an issue once you have found it is important. It can be tempting to skim the surface, find something - a nugget - and say "let me take it away and think about it, I'll get back to you". A lot of people do this because of the pressure of thinking on their feet or feeling that they need to go back to the office and reflect. They want to defer their thinking to a time when there is no pressure, no time constraints, and where they can't look silly. If you do this, you will lose momentum on the issue. Rather than feeling the need to find a full-blown solution, discuss what a good outcome might look like and discuss several possible ways forward.

This is about being creative and thinking laterally. It is not about going away and doing more research or analysis. The idea here is to keep the conversation flowing, to come up with some quick wins that can be implemented, and to build on the momentum that you have already generated.

So the key takeaways from this chapter are:

- Keep the focus on the future
- Help the client find their own solutions
- Be supportive and positive

- Deep dive into an issue once you have found it

- Get the client to articulate the consequences of not fixing the issue

- Share your ideas and thoughts freely on the issue at the right time (not too early)

- Come up with a range of possible solutions

- Keep the conversation flowing, come up with some quick wins that can be implemented, and build on the momentum that you have generated.

CHAPTER 17: GO OUT AND BUILD TRUSTED RELATIONSHIPS

You can now build relationships that are based on trust. You have the ability to create bonds with others that are built on a foundation of honesty and respect. With this newfound power, you can take your professional interactions to a whole new level!

You can excel as a technical consultant by selling your expertise, and you can succeed as a salesman by selling your company's products. But if you become a trusted advisor, the sky's the limit when it comes to the potential applications of this new found power, so make sure to use it wisely!

You may need to explain to your firm what kind of adviser you want to be. That you want to be a trusted adviser, and that being a trusted adviser requires more than just technically sound advice. It requires deep understanding of the client's business, and it demands mutual trust and respect.

There is a clear business case for being a trusted advisor rather than a salesman. Salespeople are a dime a dozen, but trusted advisers are rare. And the rewards for being a trusted adviser can be great, both professionally and personally. Don't be scared to tell your firm that you believe this. After all, they hired you because they believe in your potential. Now it's time to live up to that potential!

This is your chance to set yourself apart from the competition. To become the go-to person that clients seek out when they need help making tough decisions. So make sure you're ready for it!

So let's recap...

Remember, start by knowing yourself. What are your strengths? What is your personality? What do you enjoy doing? What are you passionate about?

Go out and curate your network. Find the people who you can trust, and who will trust you in return.

Sell the relationship to your client, not the product or service. This is the key to becoming a trusted advisor. If you can build a strong relationship of trust with your client, they will be more likely to come to you for advice in the future.

Understand your clients' personalities and their agendas. What motivates them? What are their goals? What do they need in order to achieve those goals? When you know the answers to these questions, you'll be able to give them the advice **they** need, not just the advice *you* want to give.

Become comfortable with having strategic and unstructured meetings. This is where the magic of being a trusted advisor happens. In these meetings, you'll be able to build trust and rapport with your clients, and they'll be more likely to confide in you and seek your advice.

Finally, always keep learning. The world is constantly changing, and so is the business landscape. To be a trusted advisor, you need to stay ahead of the curve.

So there you have it! These are the key steps to becoming a trusted advisor. It's actually quite easy when you know how.

www.ingramcontent.com/pod-product-compliance
Lightning Source LLC
Chambersburg PA
CBHW050245220526
45465CB00002B/562